VOLUME 001

Amazing_Agent

LUNA

art by Shiei

story by Nunzio DeFilippis
and Christina Weir

[CONFIDENTIAL]

D0833569

Amazing_Agent

LUNA

VOLUME 1

story by **Nunzio DeFilippis**
& Christina Weir

art by **Shiei**

STAFF CREDITS

toning	**Jay Jimenez**
background assists	**Roland Amago**
lettering	**Nicky Lim**
graphic design	**Culture Crash**
cover design	**Nicky Lim**
assistant editor	**Adam Arnold**
editor	**Jason DeAngelis**
publisher	**Seven Seas Entertainment**

ISBN 1-933164-36-0

Printed in Canada

First printing: December, 2006

10 9 8 7 6 5 4 3 2 1

AMAZING AGENT LUNA - VOLUME 1

File 01
AMAZING AGENT

7

UNLESS SHE WANTED OUR *FIRST* MEETING TO BE IN *PRIVATE.*

OKAY... THIS IS *ODD.*

DID I *IMAGINE* HER?

OH WELL... THERE ARE MANY GIRLS IN PARIS...

13

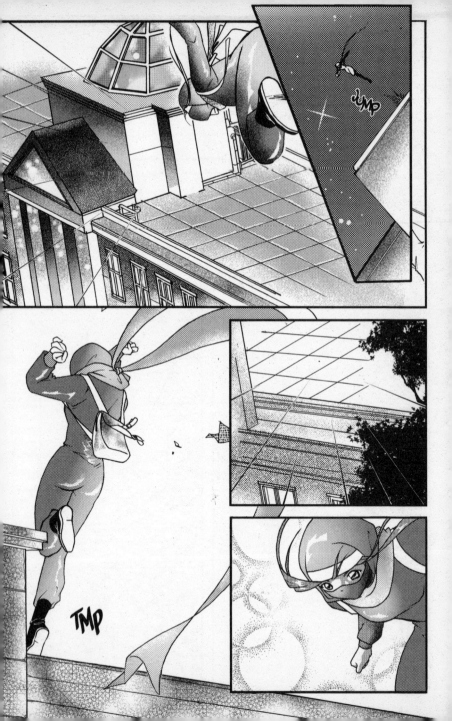

SO FAR, SO GOOD.

NOBODY'S *NOTICED* ME.

WOW...

LOOK AT THE COUNT'S OFFICE...

OKAY, HERE WE GO.

SOMEBODY'S GOT A LITTLE TOO MUCH *MONEY* TO BURN.

17

<HUMBLE OFFICE, INDEED.>

<FOR THE *USUAL* FEE.>

<*COUNT* VON BRUCKEN, I WOULD LIKE NOTHING MORE THAN TO *HELP* YOU.>

<ARE YOU INTERESTED IN HELPING ME WITH PROJECT SCION?>

<EXCELLENT.>

<...THEN LET US GO SEE ABOUT GETTING YOU A RETAINER...>

<...SO YOU CAN START WORK *IMMEDIATELY*.>

I WONDER WHO THAT *OTHER* MAN WAS WITH THE COUNT?

I SHOULD PROBABLY WAIT TIL THE COAST IS *CLEAR*.

SLAM!

23

25

TMP

GULP!

STOMP STOMP STOMP STOMP

PERHAPS I WAS A BIT HASTY...

GUARDS!

...

27

IT'S ONE GIRL! DO SOMETHING YOU MORONS!

30

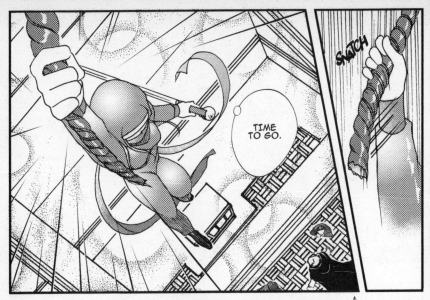

31

AGENT LUNA, THIS MISSION WAS A COMPLETE AND UTTER *FAILURE*.

YOU *HAD* COUNT HEINRICH VON BRUCKEN IN YOUR SIGHTS AND YOU DID *NOTHING* BUT *RUN*.

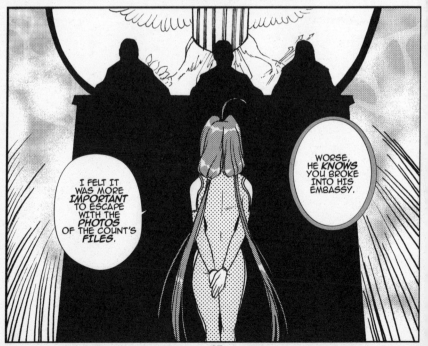

I FELT IT WAS MORE *IMPORTANT* TO ESCAPE WITH THE *PHOTOS* OF THE COUNT'S *FILES*.

WORSE, HE *KNOWS* YOU BROKE INTO HIS EMBASSY.

YES.
BECAUSE
I 'KID'
OFTEN.

Dr. ANDY COLLINS, Phd

YOU'RE
KIDDING
ME?

SHE WAS
REALLY
CRYING?

BUT IT'S PERFECTLY *NATURAL*. SHE'S *FIFTEEN*. SHE LOOKS UP TO YOU.

BAWLING. I CAN'T HAVE MY AGENTS BAWLING LIKE THAT. IT JUST ISN'T *DONE*.

MAYBE IT'S THE *ISOLATION* IN WHICH YOU RAISED HER. OR MAYBE IT'S THE *GENETIC* ENGINEERING.

MAYBE THAT'S THE *PROBLEM*. HER MOODS ARE LIKE ANY OTHER TEENAGER'S, BUT MORE *EXTREME*.

NATURAL FOR A FIFTEEN YEAR OLD, SURE. *NOT* NATURAL FOR A SPECIALLY BRED, SPECIALLY TRAINED *SECRET AGENT*.

WE KNEW THIS WOULD COME. SHE'S GOING TO GO THROUGH SOME *ROUGH* EMOTIONAL TIMES.

KNOWN TO THE REST OF THE WORLD AS *ADOLESCENCE*.

EITHER WAY, IT'S A *PROBLEM*. I NEED HER IN THE FIELD *NOW*.

AND I MUST SAY, MY ADOLESCENCE WAS NOT NEARLY SO ROUGH.

YOU WERE BROUGHT HERE, DR. COLLINS, TO *HANDLE* THOSE 'ROUGH' TIMES.

SLAM

THAT EXPLAINS A LOT ABOUT YOU.

EVEN IF YOU ACT THAT WAY SOMETIMES.

HOWEVER, REMEMBER THAT YOU WERE *NOT* BORN IN A TEST TUBE, NOR RAISED BY THE U.S. *GOVERNMENT* IN A SECRET HIDDEN BASE.

42

YOU'VE SEEN WHAT WE HAVE IN MIND FOR HER, WHAT HER NEXT MISSION IS.

THAT IS WHY *YOU* WILL BE JOINING ME FOR THIS MISSION.

IT'LL TEAR HER APART.

YES, AND SHE'S NOT *READY.* HER OUTBURST TODAY IS *PROOF.*

IT DOESN'T MATTER. VON BRUCKEN'S FILES *ALL* LINK BACK TO THIS ONE PLACE. SHE HAS TO *INFILTRATE.*

AS I SAID, I NEVER KID.

YOU AND ME? IN THE FIELD? TOGETHER?

YOU'RE KIDDING?

TOMORROW. BE READY. WE'RE SENDING HER IN.

43

WE'RE SENDING YOU *IN* BECAUSE *EVERY* FILE YOU BROUGHT US WAS OF SOMEONE IN *THERE.*

WE DON'T THINK THEY *ALL* WORK FOR VON BRUCKEN.

HEY, MAYBE NONE OF THEM DO. THEY MAY JUST BE *NICE* AND *NORMAL.*

GET TO *KNOW* THEM. FIND OUT IF THEY WORK FOR THE COUNT. OR, IF NOT, WHY HE'S INTERESTED IN THEM.

DON'T WORRY. YOU'RE GOOD AT THIS. YOU'LL DO *FINE.* THEY'LL ALL *LIKE* YOU.

44

File 02
NOBEL HIGH

49

50

HEY THERE... SORRY ABOUT ELIZABETH.

SHE'S HAVING A BAD DAY.

RAZZIN-FRAZZIN-PLASTIC--

SLUM ON YOUR OWN TIME. OLIVER RIGGS IS *NOT* WORTHY OF *MINE*.

FRANCESCA! WE'RE WALKING HERE.

HER BIRTHDAY. WHEN THE NEW FALL FASHIONS COME OUT.

WHEN DOES SHE EVER HAVE *GOOD* DAYS?

HEY! WHERE'D THE *NEW* GIRL GO?

YEAH. 'SEE YOU LATER.' NOT LIKELY.

GOTTA GO. SEE YOU LATER.

PRINCIPAL

I FIND THAT THE MORE *INVOLVED* THE PARENTS ARE, THE MORE *FULFILLED* THE CHILD IS.

THANK YOU BOTH FOR COMING.

EXCUSE ME, PRINCIPAL OHLINGER, BUT I GO BY MS. KAJIWARA.

OH, I AM *SO* SORRY.

NOW... MR. AND MRS. COLLINS, WHY DON'T YOU TELL ME ABOUT YOUR DAUGHTER?

GOOD. NOT THAT IT WOULD BE A *PROBLEM.* ANY FAMILY IS A *GOOD* FAMILY IF IT HAS *LOVE.*

BUT YOU TWO *ARE* MARRIED...?

OF COURSE. HAPPILY MARRIED.

VERY... HAPPILY MARRIED.

52

I USED TO LISTEN TO YOUR RADIO SHOW ALL THE TIME. WHY DID IT GO OFF THE AIR?

I WENT INTO *PRIVATE* PRACTICE.

A VERY *WISE* WAY OF TEACHING.

WE JUST LIKE TO KNOW OF ANY HOME SITUATIONS SO WE CAN TAILOR THE LEARNING EXPERIENCE FOR EACH CHILD.

I SEE... THAT'S A REAL SHAME.

NOW, IS THERE ANYTHING WE SHOULD KNOW ABOUT LUNA?

THANK YOU, DR. COLLINS. FROM YOU, THAT'S *HIGH* PRAISE.

WE JUST WANT TO MAKE SURE THAT THE... *INTERPERSONAL* SITUATIONS... DO NOT GET IN THE WAY OF HER STUDIES.

JENNIFER AND I HAVE... HOME-SCHOOLED LUNA UP TIL NOW.

SHE'S NEW TO THE SOCIAL NUANCES OF HIGH SCHOOL.

LET ME EXPLAIN HOW NOBEL HIGH WORKS. THIS IS THE FINEST HIGH SCHOOL IN THE COUNTRY.

AND TO US, EVERY CHILD HAS A STORY ALL THEIR OWN.

THE STUDENTS HERE ARE THE CHILDREN OF DIPLOMATS, SCIENTISTS AND LEADERS FROM ALL AROUND THE WORLD.

YOU NEEDN'T SELL US ON THE SCHOOL. OUR DAUGHTER IS ALREADY HERE.

FITTING IN IS DIFFICULT FOR *ALL* OF THEM. LUNA'S SITUATION ISN'T ANY *DIFFERENT.*

CLASS, WE HAVE A NEW STUDENT TODAY.

I THINK WE'LL HAVE LUNA UP TO SPEED SOCIALLY SPEAKING, IN NO TIME.

THIS IS LUNA COLLINS.

SHE JUST TRANSFERRED TO NOBEL HIGH AND WE SHOULD ALL MAKE HER FEEL WELCOME.

LUNA, WHY DON'T YOU TELL US SOMETHING ABOUT YOURSELF?

ELIZABETH WESTBROOK, THAT IS *NOT* HOW WE MAKE PEOPLE FEEL WELCOME.

YEAH, LIKE WHERE DID YOU GET THOSE *SHOES?*

I MEAN, FOR SOMETHING TO BE *RETRO* IT NEEDS TO BE AT LEAST TEN YEARS OLD, NOT LAST SEASON'S STYLE.

IS SOMETHING *WRONG* WITH MY SHOES?

YOU'RE *FINE*, LUNA.

HA HA HA HA HA HA HA

I CAN GO HOME AND CHANGE THEM.

FIND YOURSELF AN EMPTY SEAT AND WE'LL GET CLASS STARTED.

NO NEED TO CHANGE.

56

AND THIS IS AN *EXPENSIVE* BAG. IT NEEDS ITS OWN CHAIR.

SORRY, SHE DID SAY *EMPTY*.

YOU CAN SIT OVER HERE.

PSST... LUNA...

BEFORE YOU GO, I'D LIKE YOU TO MEET ARISTOTLE, THE SCHOOL MASCOT.

OH DEAR... HE'S... *ASLEEP*.

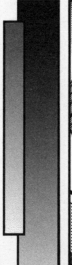

EVEN THOUGH I HAVE BAD SHOES?

I'M SURE YOU DO.

BUT, OTHER THAN THAT, I THINK THIS HAS BEEN REMARKABLY *PRODUCTIVE.* I'M GLAD YOU CAME IN.

I LIKE TO THINK THAT AT NOBEL HIGH, WHEN A CHILD ENROLLS, THE WHOLE FAMILY ENROLLS.

I, HOWEVER, WOULD PREFER YOU STICK TO THE STUDENTS AND LEAVE MY HOME LIFE OUT OF IT.

PRINCIPAL OHLINGER, I'M SURE THERE ARE MANY WHO APPRECIATE YOUR HANDS-ON, NEW AGE APPROACH TO EDUCATION.

IF I MAY... I SENSE A LITTLE... TENSION BETWEEN YOU AND YOUR HUSBAND.

IS EVERYTHING *OKAY* AT HOME BECAUSE—

YOU'RE ENJOYING THIS, AREN'T YOU?

A LITTLE.

JENNIFER, DEAR... WE'VE TAKEN UP ENOUGH OF PRINCIPAL OHLINGER'S TIME. WE SHOULD *GO.*

PLEASE FORGIVE ME IF I'VE OVERSTEPPED ANY BOUNDS.

AND DON'T WORRY ABOUT US. THERE'S PLENTY OF *LOVE* IN OUR MARRIAGE.

NOT AT ALL. NICE TO MEET YOU.

61

WHY AREN'T YOU RUNNING, COLLINS?
I'M DONE, MR. DREYFUS. FIVE LAPS.
I SAID FIVE LAPS IN TEN MINUTES.
IT DOESN'T TAKE ME TEN MINUTES. THIS WAS EASY.
I WON'T BE HAVING ANYONE SLACKING OFF IN MY CLASS. GIVE ME FIVE MORE LAPS!
BUT—
KIDS...

CLUNK

OW! HEY, I SAID I' WAS *SORRY*.

SORRY ABOUT YOUR LUNCH.

FOOD SUCKS HERE ANYWAY.

WHOA...

THERE SHE IS AGAIN.

OKAY, OLIVER... TIME TO MAKE YOUR *MOVE*. SHE'S TOO *NEW* TO THE SCHOOL TO REALIZE THAT NO ONE *LIKES* YOU.

HEY THERE.

SO.... YOU'RE THE *NEW* GIRL, RIGHT?

AND MY SHOES ARE OUT OF FASHION AND I THINK I'M SOME GIRL NAMED MARION JONES, WHATEVER THAT MEANS! AND MY MOM'S A SECRETARY!

YES! I'M THE NEW GIRL!

ANYTHING *ELSE* YOU WANT TO ADD?

I MEAN, IF YOUR MOM *IS* A SECRETARY, THAT'S COOL.

HEY, IT'S OKAY.

MY DAD IS A SECURITY GUARD AT THE U.N. AND THAT'S THE ONLY REASON I'M HERE AT THIS SCHOOL.

YOU WERE EATING ALONE AND I—

MR. RIGGS!

OH, I'M SORRY, I THOUGHT YOU CAME TO MAKE FUN OF THE NEW GIRL.

NO, 'COURSE NOT.

YOU'RE IN *BIG* TROUBLE, BUSTER.

HOW MANY TIMES HAVE I TOLD YOU *NOT* TO SKATEBOARD IN THE SCHOOL?

AND CROWDED WITH PEOPLE!

BUT THAT WAS IN THE HALLWAYS WHICH WERE CROWDED WITH PEOPLE. THIS IS THE LUNCHROOM. IT'S WIDE OPEN AND--

LET'S GO.

MARION JONES IS AN OLYMPIC RUNNER, BY THE WAY.

SO AT LEAST THEY THOUGHT YOU WERE *FAST*.

HEY, THE NEW GIRL JUST GOT OLIVER IN TROUBLE.

SLAM

TALK

LAUGH

CHATTER

GOSSIP

LAUGH

I WONDER HOW SHE DID.

68

LUNA! WHAT ABOUT YOUR REPORT?

I SAID I DON'T LIKE IT.

BUT YOU'VE GOT A BEAUTIFUL BEDROOM ON THE SECOND FLOOR. LOTS OF SPACE...

NO ONE WOULD *TALK* TO ME. THEY ALL *HATE* ME. EXCEPT ONE BOY. HE WAS NICE. BUT THEN MR. DREYFUS TOOK HIM AWAY!

I DON'T *HAVE* A REPORT.

I TOLD YOU SHE WASN'T READY—

DON'T SAY A WORD.

SLAM

MAYBE MR. DREYFUS WORKS FOR COUNT VON BRUCKEN! HE'S CERTAINLY *MEAN* ENOUGH.

AREN'T YOU FRIENDS WITH THAT GIRL WHO HATES ME?

I'M FRANCESCA. YOU'RE IN MY SCIENCE CLASS.

HI.

HOW DOES SHE ENFORCE IT? DOES SHE HAVE **SOLDIERS**?

SOLDIERS? NO SOLDIERS. SHE ENFORCES IT BY MAKING EVERYONE ELSE MISERABLE.

NO... SHE'S JUST SOCIALLY ON TOP AND HAS TO WORRY ABOUT EVERY NEW STUDENT THREATENING THAT.

ELIZABETH DOESN'T HATE YOU. SHE'S JUST... TOUGH ON NEW KIDS. SHE RULES THIS SCHOOL AND YOU MIGHT THREATEN--

RULES? HOW? LIKE A DICTATOR?

YEAH, KINDA LIKE A DICTATOR.

I AM SO TIRED OF EVERYONE TALKING ABOUT--

HEY, CHECK OUT THE NEW KID!

...ME.

WELL CONGRATULATIONS. YOU'RE NOT THE NEW KID ANYMORE.

THE BOY FROM PARIS!

OH, I HEARD ABOUT HIM. WE'VE BEEN WAITING FOR THIS ONE. HE'S GOING TO MAKE THINGS *VERY* INTERESTING AROUND HERE.

IT'S *SUCH A SCANDAL*.

WHY? WHO IS HE?

IN YOUR DREAMS

SO, CONTROL SHOULD BE THE TOTAL SEXY LIBRARIAN. BECAUSE THERE'S NOTHING SEXIER THAN THAT STERN, TEACHER-TYPE. YOU KNOW WHAT I MEAN?

TAK TAK

HELLO? WIFE HERE.

AND YOU KNOW WHAT ELSE? WE SHOULD TRY TO GET SHIEI TO DRAW A NAUGHTY NURSE. THIS BOOK NEEDS A NAUGHTY NURSE!

BONK!

WRITING PROCESS

AND THEN LUNA LEAPS INTO THE AIR, DOING AN AMAZING SOMERSAULT, GRABBING THE FLAGPOLE WHILE SHE DODGES SHURIKEN!

UH-HUH.

TAK TAK

SHE BOUNCES OFF THE NINJA'S HEAD, RIGHT THROUGH THE WINDOW! WHAT'S A GOOD SOUND EFFECT FOR BOUNCING OFF A NINJA'S HEAD?

I DON'T KNOW... MAYBE--

SPROING! GOOD IDEA! LET'S USE SPROING.

COOL. GOT IT. WE'RE DONE.

HUH? LET ME TAKE A QUICK LOOK. BE RIGHT OUT.

WHAT'S THIS?!!! THIS ISN'T WHAT I SAID-- I MEAN, WHAT WE WROTE!

CHRISTIE!!!

File 03
BAD BOY

YOU HAVE TO WORK IT. IT'S NOT LIKE HE'D JUST WALK UP TO ANY OLD GIRL AND SAY HI.

UM... ELIZABETH...

I BET HE'S WONDERING ABOUT ME RIGHT NOW.

84

SO, UH... WELL, JUST REMEMBER THAT.

YEAH, WELL, YOU MAY BE WAY COOLER THAN ME, BUT I SAW LUNA FIRST.

SO, NEW GUY, HUH?

I JUST... I HAVE NEVER BEEN TO PARIS. HE CLEARLY THINKS I'M SOMEONE ELSE.

PANT PANT

WHY DID YOU LEAVE? THE CUTEST GUY *EVER* COMES TO NOBEL HIGH, SEEKS YOU OUT AND YOU WALK AWAY?

WHAT BOOK?

LUNA! THAT'S THE OLDEST TRICK IN THE BOOK.

HOW TO PICK UP GIRLS 101. "HAVE WE MET?" IT'S JUST A LINE.

IT GIVES YOU A REASON TO TALK TO SOMEONE.

REALLY? SO YOU DON'T THINK HE RECOGNIZED ME?

NO. IT WAS TOTALLY A LINE.

THAT'S A RELIEF.

COME ON. WE'LL BE LATE FOR CLASS.

FRANCESCA? WHERE CAN I BUY THIS HOW TO BOOK?

....

RRRRRRING!

UH... LUNA! IT'S NOT A REAL BOOK.

AND SOMEONE NEEDS TO MAKE SURE SHE EATS.

WE HAVE A COVER TO MAINTAIN. YOU ARE MY *WIFE*. LUNA IS MY *DAUGHTER*.

YOU WILL CALL ME CONTROL.

CONTINUE, LUNA. TELL US ABOUT YOUR DAY AT SCHOOL.

RELAX. WE CAN KILL TWO BIRDS WITH ONE STONE.

NERVOUS? WHY?

SORRY. SO I WAS REALLY NERVOUS WHEN I SAW HIM.

WOW. THIS IS REALLY GOOD.

LUNA, PLEASE CONTINUE YOUR REPORT.

OH... DID I FORGET TO MENTION THE PART WHERE I RAN INTO HIM BOTH BEFORE AND AFTER BREAKING INTO THE EMBASSY?

WELL.... I WASN'T SURE IF HE'D RECOGNIZE ME FROM PARIS.

PARIS?

I DIDN'T *KNOW* HE WAS VON BRUCKEN'S SON. HE WAS JUST A BOY.

WHAT?! YOUR COVER COULD BE SERIOUSLY COMPROMISED!

JENNIFER... YOU'RE NOT HELPING HERE.

I'M SORRY. I JUST... IT DIDN'T SEEM *IMPORTANT* AT THE TIME.

LUNA, WHY DIDN'T YOU TELL US ABOUT SEEING HIM BEFORE?

90

HE THOUGHT I LOOKED FAMILIAR.

BUT I TOLD HIM I'D NEVER BEEN TO PARIS.

FAIR ENOUGH. NOW WHAT HAPPENED TODAY AT SCHOOL?

GOOD, THAT'S GOOD. AND DID HE BELIEVE YOU?

SHE SAYS IT'S PART OF SOME DATING PLAYBOOK BOYS HAVE.

AH, YES... I REMEMBER THE PLAYBOOK.

I THINK SO. THIS OTHER GIRL TOLD ME HE DIDN'T RECOGNIZE ME, THAT HE WAS ONLY TRYING TO TALK TO ME.

THEN WE'RE FINE.

YOU REALIZE THAT'S NOT A LITERAL BOOK, LUNA?

OF COURSE I DO.

BRRRING

ARE YOU GOING TO LUNCH, JONAH? WE COULD EAT TOGETHER?

THAT CLASS WAS SO BORING, RIGHT, JONAH?

YOU LOOK SMART, JONAH. MAYBE YOU COULD HELP ME WITH THE HOMEWORK?

HE'S NOT GOING TO LUNCH LIKE EVERYONE ELSE. WHAT COULD HE BE UP TO?

NOT RIGHT NOW. I HAVE SOMETHING TO DO.

94

100

LOOKING AT THE OWL.
RIGHT. DUMB QUESTION. OKAY, WHY ARE YOU LOOKING AT THE OWL?
I THINK HE'S COOL.
YEAH, I'M JUST NOT SEEING IT. HE'S JUST... SLEEPING.
HE'S NOCTURNAL. A CREATURE OF THE NIGHT. I LIKE THAT. BESIDES, HE'S ONLY HALF ASLEEP.
WATCH HIM, YOU'LL SEE. HE KNOWS WE'RE HERE.
OKAY...
I THINK I'LL LEAVE YOU TWO ALONE.

TELL ME ABOUT HER.

YEAH. ME AND HER, WE GO WAY BACK.

YOU'RE FRIENDS WITH LUNA.

WEREN'T YOU LISTENING YESTERDAY WHEN I TOLD YOU I SAW HER FIRST?

NOT REALLY, NO.

DUDE, I AM *SO* NOT GIVING YOU THE SCOOP ON HER.

ME? SHE TALKS TO ME. GOTTA GO.

IF SHE'S NOT TALKING TO YOU, MAYBE THERE'S A REASON.

MAYBE.

TODAY WE ARE GOING TO TALK ABOUT GREGOR MENDEL...

...AND HIS STUDIES OF GENETICS.

CAN I USE THE BATHROOM?

DR. WARREN?

JONAH WOULDN'T DO THIS.

I'M TELLING YOU, IT WAS THAT NEW GUY.

OH YEAH! I SAW HIM STARING AT ARISTOTLE TODAY LIKE HE WAS HIS GIRLFRIEND OR SOMETHING.

THAT GUY'S NOT RIGHT IN THE HEAD.

I WOULD REALLY LIKE THAT, BUT I CAN'T. MY... PARENTS ARE WAITING FOR ME.

WHATEVER. I'LL BET HE TURNS UP TOMORROW.

HEY, LUNA, WANT TO COME OVER THIS AFTERNOON?

THAT'S SO WEIRD. WHY WOULD SOMEONE TAKE AN OWL?

A VERY GOOD QUESTION. MAYBE WE SHOULD INVESTIGATE.

HELLO, I'M HOME!

HEY, LUNA. HOW WAS SCHOOL?

GOOD, IT WAS ACTUALLY GOOD.

FRANCESCA INVITED ME TO GO SHOPPING THIS WEEKEND. SHE THINKS JONAH MIGHT ASK ME OUT.

AND THAT'S GOOD, RIGHT? BECAUSE THEN I CAN REALLY KEEP AN EYE ON HIM--

OWL? WHAT'S GOING ON?

ARE YOU GOING TO TELL US ABOUT THE OWL?

AND?

AND WHAT?

OH YEAH. SOMEONE TOOK ARISTOTLE. BUT FRANCESCA THINKS HE'LL TURN UP TOMORROW.

YOU'RE KIDDING, RIGHT? YOU THINK A MISSING MASCOT FALLS UNDER THE AGENCY'S BUSINESS?

DOES SHE? AND WHERE DID FRANCESCA STUDY INVESTIGATIVE SKILLS? LUNA, YOU'RE NOT FOCUSING.

NO, CONTROL. I'LL BE BETTER. I ALMOST HAD A CHANCE TO STEAL JONAH'S NOTEBOOK TODAY.

I THINK THAT THE SON OF ONE OF THE MOST *DANGEROUS* MEN OUT THERE ARRIVES AT THIS SCHOOL AND THE VERY NEXT DAY SOMETHING WEIRD HAPPENS.

I THINK MY AGENT HAS FORGOTTEN *EVERYTHING* SHE'S LEARNED.

I'M JUST TRYING TO BLEND IN.

LUNA, WE HAVE NO INTEL ON PROJECT SCION AND YOUR IDENTITY MAY BE COMPROMISED.

INSTEAD OF THE MISSION, YOU ARE FOCUSED ON BOYS AND SHOPPING.

NO, LUNA. YOUR PERFORMANCE IS COMPLETELY UNACCEPTABLE. THIS WAS A MISTAKE.

WE'RE PULLING YOU OUT OF NOBEL HIGH.

File 04
FIRST CRUSH

113

114

HI. WHAT'S GOING ON?

LUNA?

UH.... YEAH.

COOL. GOT THE RIGHT NUMBER THEN. THIS IS FRANCESCA. FROM SCHOOL.

OH... WELL... TONIGHT MIGHT NOT—

SINCE YOU'RE NEW AND PROBABLY STILL CATCHING UP, I THOUGHT MAYBE WE COULD STUDY TOGETHER FOR DR. WARREN'S SCIENCE CLASS. TONIGHT?

DON'T YOU *EVER* CALL ME STUPID AGAIN, YOU NAIVE NEW-AGE...

SO, WHAT ABOUT TOMORROW THEN?

LUNA, WE NEED TO TALK.

KINDA. YEAH.

OH. ARE YOUR PARENTS FIGHTING?

MINE FIGHT ALL THE TIME TOO. JUST REMEMBER THAT IT'S NEVER REALLY ABOUT YOU.

CLICK

I GOTTA GO, FRANCESCA.

THAT'S COOL. SEE YOU AT SCHOOL TOMORROW.

I HOPE SO.

IT HAS BEEN MADE CLEAR TO ME THAT IN THE INTEREST OF YOUR FUTURE TRAINING AS AN AGENT...

I GET TO HAVE FRIENDS?

AND THAT HIGH SCHOOL IS THE BEST PLACE FOR THAT.

...WE SHOULD PERHAPS LET YOU COME TO TERMS WITH YOUR ADOLESCENCE.

WHILE THERE IS GREAT *RISK* IN JONAH VON BRUCKEN FIGURING OUT WHO YOU ARE, THERE IS ALSO A LOT TO BE GAINED FROM GETTING *CLOSE* TO HIM.

ARE YOU KIDDING?

FRIENDS ARE A VITAL SOURCE OF INTEL. HAVING A NETWORK IN PLACE CAN BE THE DIFFERENCE BETWEEN SUCCESS AND FAILURE.

YOU *NEED* TO HAVE FRIENDS, LUNA. EVERYONE DOES.

YEAH. *THAT'S* WHY IT'S IMPORTANT.

ELIZABETH! CHECK *THAT* OUT.

SOMETHING NEEDS TO BE *DONE* ABOUT THAT.

YEAH...

WOW, THAT REALLY IS GREAT. GOOD FOR YOU!

GOOD FOR LUNA WHAT?

I'VE DECIDED.

GREAT! WHAT DID YOU DECIDE?

I'M GOING TO TALK TO JONAH.

OH, YEAH... THE WORD IS *BAD*. HE'S JUST *BAD NEWS*. *BAD, BAD, BAD.*

THAT'S *NOT* GOOD. THAT'S THE *OPPOSITE* OF GOOD. WHAT'S THE WORD I'M LOOKING FOR?

LUNA'S GOING TO TALK TO JONAH.

HI, OLIVER!

NO! HE'S OWL-OBSESSED AND THERE'S A MISSING OWL.

SOUNDS GOOD TO ME.

HELLO?? THE GUY'S PROBABLY A CRIMINAL. REALLY DANGEROUS.

HE'S JONAH VON BRUCKEN. AS IN BRUCKENSTEIN. AS IN, *ROGUE NATION*. HE'S ALL BROODY AND MYSTERIOUS AND DANGEROUS.

WHY?

NO, I'M GOOD. WHERE WAS I...?

TALKING ABOUT A CRIMINAL, I THINK.

THUM?!

OLIVER! LOOK OUT!

OLIVER FAWL DOWN, GO BOOM...

HE SOUNDS LIKE BAD NEWS. TELL ME WHO HE IS AND I'LL AVOID HIM.

YEAH, WELL.... I'D JUST AVOID *MIRRORS* IF I WERE YOU.

I'D BETTER MAKE SURE OLIVER DIDN'T... HURT HIMSELF.

YOU TWO... TALK.

FRANCESCA... WAIT.

WE JUST KEEP RUNNING INTO EACH OTHER.

I WASN'T IN PARIS!

WHO SAID ANYTHING ABOUT YOU FOLLOWING ME. I JUST SAID I SAW YOU IN THE LIBRARY, AND IT WAS... NICE.

I WASN'T FOLLOWING YOU. I LIKE BOOKS. I WANTED A BOOK.

YEAH... I GOT THAT. BUT YOU *WERE* IN THE LIBRARY YESTERDAY.

YEAH. NICE IS GOOD.

OH. NICE IS GOOD. RIGHT?

LUNA COLLINS! WHAT ARE YOU DOING HANGING AROUND A BOY LIKE JONAH VON BRUCKEN?

AND DO YOU *KNOW* WHAT TALKING LEADS TO?

...MORE TALKING?

BUT—

DON'T YOU GIVE ME SASS, BOY! DON'T YOU TWO HAVE CLASSES TO ATTEND?

WE'RE JUST TALKING.

124

125

GET DOWN!

I NEED TO DO SOMETHING. BUT IF ANYONE SEES ME... IF *JONAH* SEES ME...

OKAY... YOU'RE WELCOME.

I COULD HAVE TAKEN CARE OF MYSELF.

131

SCREE—URK!

A FEW MORE PASSES...

AND THAT'S...

I SHOULD ASK FRANCESCA ABOUT THE RULES OF VOLLEYBALL.

...I DON'T ACTUALLY KNOW. TWO POINTS? WHAT DO YOU CALL IT?

HMMMM....

YOU NEVER TAUGHT ME HOW TO PLAY VOLLEYBALL, BY THE WAY.

A REGRETTABLE OVERSIGHT. FOCUS, LUNA.

SO THEY FOLLOWED ME INTO THE GYM. THEY HAVE A VOLLEYBALL NET THERE.

AND WHO IS RESPONSIBLE FOR THE OWLS?

VERY WELL DONE, LUNA.

TASTE THIS.

SORRY. ANYWAY, I WRAPPED ALL THE OWLS UP INTO THE NET. AND NO ONE GOT HURT.

I DON'T KNOW YET, BUT I THINK I SHOULD INVESTIGATE MR. DREYFUS.

IS HE THE MOST LOGICAL SUSPECT?

FINE. YOU WILL INVESTIGATE THIS MR. DREYFUS.

THAT'S VERY ASTUTE OF YOU, LUNA.

IT'S GOOD, BUT IT NEEDS MORE... I DON'T KNOW, SOMETHING.

WELL, HE DOESN'T LIKE KIDS A WHOLE LOT. AND WHO TEACHES HIGH SCHOOL IF THEY DON'T LIKE KIDS?

MAN! HOW COME I'M ALWAYS FALLING WHEN I DO THIS DURING THE DAY?

TA-DA

--AROUND.

BUT THE ONE TIME I DO IT PERFECTLY, THERE'S NO ONE--

I... I LEFT MY HOMEWORK IN MY LOCKER.

BUMMER. THEY LOCK THE SCHOOL UP PRETTY TIGHT AT NIGHT. BUT I KNOW A WAY IN.

HEY, OLIVER...

HEY, LUNA!

SO WHAT HAPPENED TODAY WITH JONAH? AFTER ALL THAT FUSS WITH THE OWLS, I FORGOT TO ASK.

THIS IS A LOT OF WORK FOR HOMEWORK. YOU'RE REALLY SERIOUS ABOUT CATCHING UP QUICKLY.

HE WANTED TO PROTECT ME FROM THE OWLS. HE PUSHED ME TO THE GROUND. AND HE WAS SO CLOSE.

HE HAS BLUE EYES.

ENOUGH WITH THE SMALL TALK, PEOPLE. IN AND OUT. BEFORE ANYONE SEES US.

OH. MY. GOD. THAT'S SO *ROMANTIC!*

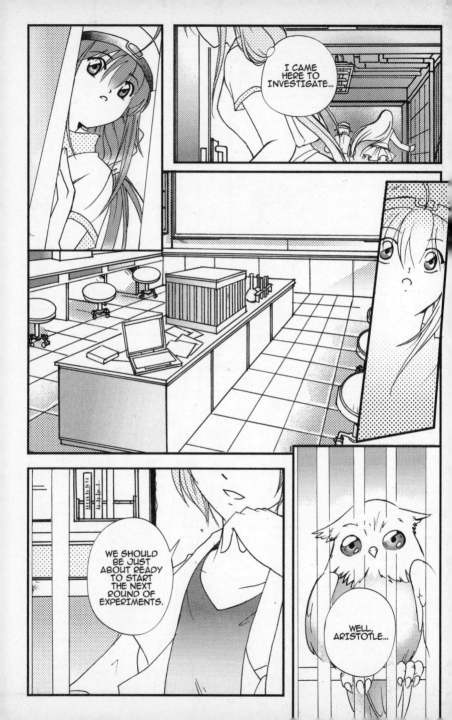

SHE'S RESPONSIBLE FOR THE OWLS?

LET'S HOPE THEY GO BETTER THAN TODAY'S FIASCO.

DR. WARREN...?

GOOD EVENING, COUNT VON BRUCKEN.

STATUS REPORT! HAVE WE MADE PROGRESS ON PROJECT SCION?

UNACCEPTABLE! THEY MUST BE INDISTINGUISHABLE FROM THE ORIGINAL.

SUPER STRONG OWLS? WHAT'S VON BRUCKEN GOT PLANNED?

TODAY'S EXPERIMENT WAS A PARTIAL SUCCESS. WHILE MY STRENGTH-ENHANCING GENE THERAPY DOES WORK, THE OWLS WERE A BIT LARGER THAN THE ORIGINAL SPECIMEN.

BEFORE? NO. THERE WILL BE *NO* TELLING. DO EITHER OF YOU KNOW THE MEANING OF *'TOP SECRET'*?

LUNA, CONSIDER WHAT A BIG THING THIS IS. YOU WERE BORN IN A LABORATORY AND RAISED TO BE A SPY. THAT'S A *LOT* TO TAKE IN.

YOU NEED TO BE SURE THEY'RE READY FOR THIS BEFORE YOU TELL THEM.

YOU WILL APPREHEND DR. WARREN AND GET OUT OF THERE BEFORE ANYONE CAN IDENTIFY YOU.

NO BUTS. LUNA, YOU WILL TAKE YOUR STEALTH GEAR TO SCHOOL TOMORROW AND AFTER CLASS YOU WILL GO BACK TO THE LAB.

UNDERSTOOD?

YES, CONTROL.

I JUST THOUGHT IT WOULD BE HELPFUL IF THEY KNEW. THEY'RE MY FRIENDS.

AND IT'S GOOD THAT YOU'RE MAKING FRIENDS. BUT--

I SHOULD USE FRANCESCA'S ADVICE.

I'LL TALK TO JONAH AND MAKE HIM LIKE ME AGAIN.

I'M GONNA TAKE OUT DR. WARREN *NOW*. THE SOONER I'M OUT OF HERE, THE BETTER.

FINE. I DON'T *CARE* IF HE GOES OUT WITH HER. I DON'T BELONG HERE ANYWAY.

I THOUGHT MAYBE WE COULD GO SEE A MOVIE FRIDAY NIGHT.

A MOVIE? YEAH, SURE. WHY NOT?

FINISHED

AMAZING ARTIST SHIEI

File 06
MISSION ACCOMPLISHED?

I WONDER WHAT'S BOTHERING HER?

THERE GOES LUNA.

ALONE.

OF COURSE.

MAY I HAVE A WORD WITH YOU, ELIZABETH?

ME RUDE? DON'T YOU KNOW THAT LUNA AND JONAH HAVE... WELL, HAVE SOMETHING GOING ON BETWEEN THEM?

AND TELL ME WHY I SHOULD CARE WHO THE NEW GIRL HAS A CRUSH ON? OR BETTER YET, WHY SHOULD *YOU* CARE?

GEEZ, FRANCESCA. RUDE MUCH?

I HAVE A JOB TO DO.

I DON'T CARE IF JONAH *DOES* HAVE BEAUTIFUL EYES.

IF DR. WARREN IS DOWN HERE, I'LL TAKE CARE OF HER.

AFTER ALL, I KNOW WHERE SHE'LL BE IN SECOND PERIOD.

IF NOT, I'LL CLEAN OUT THE LAB AND FIND HER LATER.

SCREECH!

WELL WHAT DO WE HAVE HERE? A NINJA?

DAMN BIRD!

A NINJA VERSUS A SCIENCE TEACHER... IT HARDLY SEEMS *FAIR.*

AND IT *ISN'T!*

I'LL GET HIM BACK.

159

I BROUGHT THE POLICE, MR. DREYFUS!

KIDNAPPING THE SCHOOL MASCOT IS A *SERIOUS* OFFENSE.

ARI! OH ARISTOTLE, THERE YOU ARE!

I THOUGHT WE WERE ALL *FAMILY.*

I'M VERY DISAPPOINTED IN YOU, DR. WARREN.

MY LOYALTY LIES WITH A *DIFFERENT* FAMILY.

WOW... DR. WARREN. MY MONEY WAS ON JONAH.

WE KNOW, OLIVER.

I'M JUST GLAD THEY CAUGHT HER.

WE WERE *WORRIED.*

LUNA! WHERE WERE YOU?

HEY, KNOW WHAT I HEARD? DR. WARREN TRIED TO *CLONE* ARISTOTLE.

EEWW! WHERE'D YOU HEAR THAT?

I'M FINE. WE SHOULD GO SHOPPING THIS WEEKEND.

ALRIGHT. THAT SOUNDS LIKE *FUN*.

ARE YOU OKAY FRANCESCA?

THAT'S *GROSS*.

REALLY? WHY? I MEAN, IT'S WEIRD. BUT LIFE GROWN IN A LAB IS STILL LIFE.

PRINCIPAL OHLINGER WAS TALKING TO THE COPS. THEY FOUND ALL SORTS OF EVIDENCE IN THE LAB. THEY THINK THOSE OTHER OWLS WERE CLONES.

IT'S IMMORAL. IT'S WRONG. *NOTHING* GOOD CAN COME FROM IT.

164

I'M SERIOUS. WE'VE NEVER MET, OKAY!

NO. GO AWAY, BIRD. I DON'T KNOW YOU.

GOOD MORNING, LUNA. MY ARISTOTLE DOES SEEM TO LIKE YOU.

HE DOESN'T USUALLY RESPOND TO THE STUDENTS.

HE'S SWEET. I'D BETTER GET TO CLASS.

FINE. BUT IT'S OUR *SECRET*.

168

Amazing Agent
LUNA
VOLUME 002

Nunzio DeFillipis ┃ Christina Weir ┃ Shiei

Luna's undercover work at Nobel High gets more dangerous, with the coming of the new Science teacher — a known agent of Count Von Brucken! But Luna's problems don't stop there — her friends are on the verge of discovering her secrets, and Jonah, the brooding boy of her dreams, begins dating snobbish Elizabeth, who's made it her personal mission to make Luna's life miserable.

MEMORANDUM

TO: OUR READERS
FROM: NUNZIO DEFILIPPIS AND CHRISTINA WEIR
RE: AMAZING AGENT LUNA

Amazing Agent Luna is a true story.

Seriously.

We knew a girl in high school who was a secret agent. It took a while to
figure it out, and she was very good at hiding it. But we could tell she
was different because of the odd way she reacted to every little thing. We
were also tipped off by the fact that whenever the bad guys attacked, she
was never around, but 'someone' would always save the day. Then, when it
was over, she'd be there, confused as ever.

She had never been in a social environment before and did she ever have a
rough time. Everything was new for her, and she was unprepared for her
emotions, for her first crushes, for her first love. She couldn't handle
rejection, peer pressure, cliques, snobs, or any of the parts of high
school that make it a singularly frustrating experience. But boy could she
kick butt.

Okay, we lied. The girl we knew wasn't a secret agent. We didn't know
anyone like Luna, because no-one is like Luna. We wanted to take a some-
what familiar concept - the complete innocent who is learning about the
world - and tell the story from her point of view, instead of focusing on
the people who find her, or befriend her (as many of those stories do).
Luna gets to experience everything for the first time, and she gets to do
it in high school.

But Luna isn't that unique. High school feels like alien terrain for all
of us. Everything we encounter there is new and frustrating and confusing.
And the cliques, the peer pressure, the snobs… they could drive anyone
crazy, even if they weren't genetically engineered and raised in isolated
government bases.

So Luna is everything a teenage girl must feel entering high school, only
more. She's one step removed from anyone we know, but not so different
that we don't want her to succeed in high school. Which is how we hope
you'll react to her too.

But, unlike most teens, if all goes wrong for Luna, at least she can still
kick butt.

Anyway, we hope you enjoy reading about Luna as much as we enjoyed writing
about her. Seeing her come to life under Shiei's talented pencils has been
an incredible thrill. If there is no-one in the world quite like Luna, it
might be because of Shiei, who has turned our little girl into an Amazing
Secret Agent.

CREATOR DOSSIER

WRITERS

Nunzio DeFilippis was born in New York, grew up in New York, loves New York, and lives in Los Angeles. He is a graduate of USC's screenwriting program and has written several feature films that no one will ever see, including one that was purchased by a production company that went out of business mere weeks later. After that, he started writing with Christina Weir.

Christina Weir was born in New York but spent her formative years in Boston. She has a Master's Degree in Television Production (for all the good that does) from Emerson College. She has lived in Los Angeles for the past ten years.

As a team, they have spent several years writing for television. They were on the writing staff of HBOs ARLISS for two seasons, and have worked on Disney's KIM POSSIBLE. In addition, they have written several feature films, none of which have been produced. This led them to explore the comics medium. Nunzio wrote an issue of DETECTIVE COMICS solo before collaborating with Christina on SKIN-WALKER for Oni Press. They have also written THREE STRIKES, MARIA'S WEDDING, THE TOMB and the ongoing fantasy story ONCE IN A BLUE MOON. Their work at Oni got the attention of Marvel Comics which led them to writing the relaunch of Marvel's teen mutant franchise NEW MUTANTS. This book has recently graduated to become NEW X-MEN: ACADEMY X. They've also written for DC Comics' WONDER WOMAN. Nunzio and Christina are married.

ARTIST

Shiei was grown in a laboratory some twenty odd years ago, bred from the finest artistic genes. She began drawing at an early age after learning how to hold a crayon and discovering what a good canvas stark white walls can make. She learned how to draw even better by sitting at her father's side, watching and helping him prepare visual aids for Shiei's school teacher mom. In her elementary school years, Shiei exhibited behavior that would forever alter the course of her life: she became hopelessly addicted to such tv anime as CANDY CANDY, SABER RIDERS, and DRAGON BALL Z.

In college, Shiei studied fine arts, with a major in advertising. She has never had a job in her entire life, unless you count babysitting her cousin. She currently lives in San Fernando Valley, with 11 parakeets, 6 cockatiels and 3 gold fish. When she grows up, Shiei would like to be a mad scientist.

Currently wants a Hachiko plushie

(Who's Hachiko? Check out BLADE FOR BARTER, another great Seven Seas title!)

HERE'S A SNEAK PEEK AT NUNZIO AND CHRISTINA'S VERY FIRST PROPOSAL FOR AMAZING AGENT LUNA. NOTICE HOW DIFFERENT THE TITLE WAS BACK THEN.

	SCOPE	TAB NO.

SUBJECT   ORIGINAL PROPOSAL

OPERATION: HIGHSCHOOL
A proposal for an original manga series
By Nunzio DeFilippis & Christina Weir

Operation: Highschool (name subject to change in case it's in use) is the story of Luna, the perfect secret agent. A girl grown in a lab from the finest genetic material, she has been trained since her birth fifteen years ago to be the United States government's ultimate espionage weapon. But she will get an assignment that will test her to the utmost of her capacity – high school.

Luna has just defeated the evil Count Von Brucken, but his lab makes it clear something big and scary will be going down at Nobel High, the elite high school maintained by the U.N. for the children of diplomats, scientists and other international figures.   This master plan is unspecified and will come down by graduation day for the class of 2007. Needing an agent who can work undercover at a high school, the government sends in Luna.

But the one thing Luna has not been trained to handle is her own feelings. They are powerful and out of control, your average teen, but without parents or real interaction to steer her. And worse, no one ever thought she'd need to figure them out. Putting her in high school is lighting the fuse on an emotional bomb of adolescent confusion. Especially when she starts to make friends, and have crushes, including a flirtation with Jonah, the son of Von Brucken.

ON THE FOLLOWING PAGES YOU'LL FIND N & C'S EARLY NOTES ON THE CAST AND SHIEI'S CHARACTER DESIGNS. CAN YOU DETECT ALL THE CHANGES TO THE FINAL DESIGN AND STORYLINE?

Character sketches - LUNA

~~RT~~ PRODUCED AT	DATE PRODUCED	FILE PROCESSED BY		NATURE OF REPORT
CHQ D-6				**[CLASSIFIED]**

FILE NO.

SUBJECT	ORIGINAL LUNA PROFILE	SCOPE	TAB NO.

Luna is the perfect girl. She's smart, she's strong, she's agile, she's attractive. But for a secret agent, she is a complete innocent. Luna was never allowed to be a child, spending her early years learning and training with adult agents. She is expected to be emotion free as a result, but instead, adolescence has brought all the turmoil one would expect from a teen crashing to the surface. It's lingering just under the surface until she gets assigned to Nobel High. And then it explodes. When she first arrives, her cover is that she's from the country. So she dresses as a bumpkin – in overalls, etc. Once she makes friends, she'll get a makeover to be more of a city girl. But she'll never lose that cute innocence that somehow makes her even more attractive.

Character sketches - LUNA

REPORT PRODUCED AT	DATE PRODUCED	FILE PROCESSED BY	NATURE OF REPORT
CHQ D-6			[CLASSIFIED]

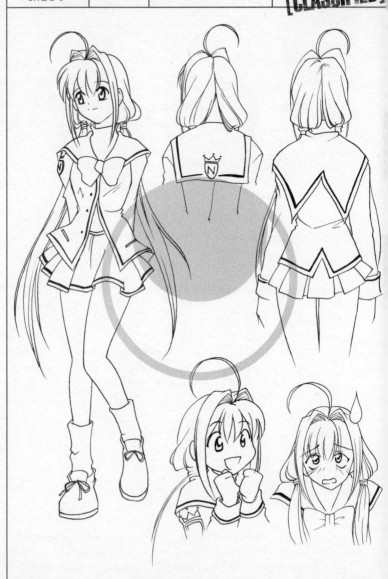

...RT PRODUCED AT	DATE PRODUCED	FILE PROCESSED BY	NATURE OF REPORT
CHQ D-6			[CLASSIFIED]

BUAHAHA!

DON'T MESS THE COPE!!!

SUBJECT ADDENDUM		SCOPE	TAB NO.

Early Von Brucken designs looked like a cross between Doctor Strange and Count Dracula.

Character sketches - COUNT HEINRICH VON BRUCKEN | FILE NO.

REPORT PRODUCED AT	DATE PRODUCED	FILE PROCESSED BY	NATURE OF REPORT
CHQ D-6			**[CLASSIFIED]**

SUBJECT	ORIGINAL VON BRUCKEN PROFILE		SCOPE	TAB NO.

Our bad guy. Count Von Brucken is a Count from the small Eastern European nation of Bruckenwald. Never heard of Bruckenwald? That's because it is basically a mountaintop in Eastern Europe - one castle ruled by the Count with an iron fist. He wants to bring the whole world under his control, but after the beginning of our story, he is in jail as a result of Luna's actions – though he never sees her face. His master plan centers on Nobel High, but no one knows why. He is evil, but like his son, there is a roguish good look to him. He's in his forties, strong and powerful. He carries himself like a king.

FILE NO.

RT PRODUCED AT	DATE PRODUCED	FILE PROCESSED BY	NATURE OF REPORT
CHQ D-6			[CLASSIFIED]

SUBJECT	ORIGINAL JONAH PROFILE		SCOPE	TAB NO.

Jonah is the handsome, mysterious brooder, equally new to Nobel High. His connection to Count Von Brucken will make him number one suspect in whatever the Count's evil plans are. But Jonah's affiliation will remain a mystery up til the end. Jonah is the type to wear a long coat and stand alone in the moonlight. In short, he's the dangerous loner that high school girls shouldn't like, but always do. His arrival at Nobel High will have all the girls swooning.

Character sketches - OLIVER RIGGS

FILE NO.

REPORT PRODUCED AT	DATE PRODUCED	FILE PROCESSED BY	NATURE OF REPORT
CHQ D-6			[CLASSIFIED

SUBJECT	ORIGINAL OLIVER PROFILE		SCOPE	TAB NO.

Oliver is the underachiever son of one of the Security personnel who keeps tabs on the United Nations. A lot of the other kids give Oliver grief because his parents aren't diplomats or geniuses. Some give him grief because he's a little dorky at times. But Oliver is reliable, good natured and a fast friend to Luna. Oliver should have that boy next door quality. While his father is a towering hulk of a man, Oliver should be pretty unremarkable in physique. Picture Oliver as the skateboarding, picked on type. He's too much fun for the dorks, and too odd for the in crowd.

RT PRODUCED AT	DATE PRODUCED	FILE PROCESSED BY	NATURE OF REPORT
CHQ D-6			[CLASSIFIED]

SUBJECT	ORIGINAL ELIZABETH PROFILE	SCOPE	TAB NO.

Elizabeth is a snooty English girl, the daughter of UN diplomat and a brillant scientist. Elizabeth is smart, beautiful and popular and she knows it. She is the stuck-up foil for Luna. Francesca and Elizabeth start out as friends but have a falling out when Francesca befriends Luna, and starts hanging out with Luna and Oliver. She's the kind of girl who hems her school skirt so short that it's practically a belt. Elizabeth loves to look good and that should be key to her look. Elizabeth is blonde.

Character sketches - FRANCESCA ALDANA

FILE NO.

REPORT PRODUCED AT	DATE PRODUCED	FILE PROCESSED BY	NATURE OF REPORT
CHQ D-6			[CLASSIFIED]

SUBJECT	ORIGINAL FRANCESCA PROFILE	SCOPE	TAB NO.

Francesca is the fifteen year old daughter of Spanish diplomats. She is all grace and charm. She runs with the beautiful people crowd of high school, but isn't as stuck-up. She's the one who takes Luna on as a project for a makeover to try to get her in with the cool kids. When the cool kids continue to reject Luna, Francesca will have to make a choice. Francesca is hip, precociously sexy and always dressed in the latest fashion with long flowy hair.

RT PRODUCED AT	DATE PRODUCED	FILE PROCESSED BY	NATURE OF REPORT
CHQ D-6			[CLASSIFIED]

SUBJECT ORIGINAL CONTROL PROFILE		SCOPE	TAB NO.

Luna's by the book, hard as nails Control Agent. Jennifer is the daughter of a Japanese businessman and a American writer. Jennifer left home after college and never returned, disappearing into the mystery life of a secret agent. She gets a new assignment when Luna does. She'll remain a control agent, but with a new codename: Mom. Jennifer is in her mid-thirties, uptight, by the book and a little too sterile. She should be a variation on the sexy librarian. Glasses, very businesslike and probably quite the hottie if she ever let her hair down.

Character sketches - DR. ANDY COLLINS

REPORT PRODUCED AT	DATE PRODUCED	FILE PROCESSED BY	NATURE OF REPORT
CHQ D-6 .			[CLASSIFIED]

FILE NO.

SUBJECT	ORIGINAL DR. ANDY PROFILE	SCOPE	TAB NO.

The government psychiatrist assigned to keep an eye on Luna when she hits her teen years. He's been saying all along that Luna needs training with her emotions, but Control never listened to him. Now that Luna's been assigned to High School, Dr. Andy will get re-assigned. He will play Luna's Dad, opposite Control, who he really can't stand. Dr. Andy is in his forties, laid back, good natured. A feel good kind of guy with a ponytail and an earring. He will love playing "Dad" to Luna because he thinks she really needs it.

[FOR YOUR EYES ONLY]

BEHIND THE SCENES

Making manga's a lot like making movies. First you start with a screenplay. Then you make storyboards based on that screenplay. The final art is then created based on the storyboards.

Let's a take an inside look at the first couple pages of Nunzio and Christina's script, and see how it was translated by Shiei into ruffs.

Luna rounds the corner and ducks into an alley. Jonah gets up from the

Nothing. It's empty save for a dumpster or two. There are fire escapes on

EXT. ROOFTOP - SAME
We're on the ROOF of one of the buildings that lined the alley. Luna is now

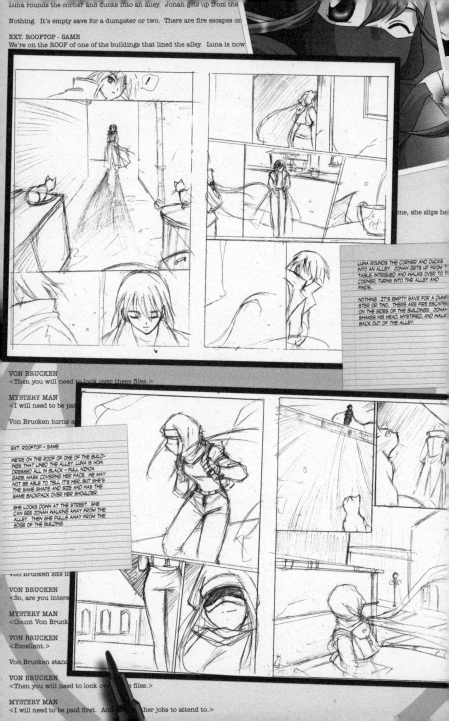

one, she slips he

LUNA ROUNDS THE CORNER AND DUCKS
INTO AN ALLEY. JONAH GETS UP FROM T
TABLE, INTRIGUED AND WALKS OVER TO T
CORNER, TURNS INTO THE ALLEY AND
FINDS...

NOTHING. IT'S EMPTY SAVE FOR A DUMP
STER OR TWO. THERE ARE FIRE ESCAPE
ON THE SIDES OF THE BUILDINGS. JONAH
SHAKES HIS HEAD, MYSTIFIED, AND WALK
BACK OUT OF THE ALLEY.

VON BRUCKEN
<Then you will need to look over these files.>

MYSTERY MAN
<I will need to be pai

Von Brucken turns a

EXT. ROOFTOP - SAME
WE'RE ON THE ROOF OF ONE OF THE BUILD-
INGS THAT LINED THE ALLEY. LUNA IS NOW
DRESSED ALL IN BLACK - FULL NINJA
GARB, MASK COVERING HER FACE. WE MAY
NOT BE ABLE TO TELL IT'S HER, BUT SHE'S
THE SAME SHAPE AND SIZE AND HAS THE
SAME BACKPACK OVER HER SHOULDER.

SHE LOOKS DOWN AT THE STREET. SHE
CAN SEE JONAH WALKING AWAY FROM THE
ALLEY. THEN SHE PULLS AWAY FROM THE
EDGE OF THE BUILDING.

Von Brucken sits in

VON BRUCKEN
<So, are you intere

MYSTERY MAN
<Count Von Bruck

VON BRUCKEN
<Excellent.>

Von Brucken stand

VON BRUCKEN
<Then you will need to look over the files.>

MYSTERY MAN
<I will need to be paid first. And   her jobs to attend to.>

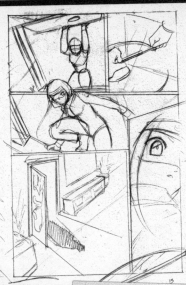

LUNA ATTACHES A SUCTION CUP TO THE WINDOW AND CUTS AROUND IT WITH A GLASS CUTTER, LIFTING A SMALL CIRCLE OF GLASS OUT. ONCE DONE, SHE SLIPS HER HAND THROUGH THE HOLE AND OPENS THE WINDOW FROM THE INSIDE.

DOWN BELOW, THE DOORS TO THE OFFICE OPEN.

INT. VON BRUCKEN'S OFFICE - SAME

COUNT VON BRUCKEN, DRESSED IN TYPICALLY ORNATE CLOTHING AND FLOWING CAPE, ENTERS. HE'S GOT HIS WALKING STICK WITH HIM. HE IS FOLLOWED IN BY A MYSTERY MAN. (SHIE, THIS GUY WON'T COME UP AGAIN UNTIL VOLUME 2, BUT WILL BE A BIG BAD GUY IN VOLUME 2. WE'LL SEND AN E-MAIL REGARDING HIS DESIGN)

VON BRUCKEN SITS IN THE CHAIR BEHIND THE DESK, THEN BRINGS HIS CAPE UP OVER THE ARM OF THE CHAIR WITH A FLOURISH. THE MYSTERY MAN STANDS IN FRONT OF THE DESK.

VON BRUCKEN
(SO, ARE YOU INTERESTED IN HELPING ME WITH PROJECT SCION?)

MYSTERY MAN
(COUNT VON BRUCKEN, I WOULD LIKE NOTHING MO... THAN TO HELP YOU. FOR THE USUAL FEE.)

VON BRUCKEN
(EXCELLENT)

VON BRUCKEN STANDS UP, DISENTANGLING HIS CA... FROM THE CHAIR WITH ANOTHER FLOURISH. HE MOVES TO A FILE CABINET IN THE CORNER.

VON BRUCKEN
(THEN YOU WILL NEED TO LOOK OVER THESE FILES)

MYSTERY MAN
(I WILL NEED TO BE PAID FIRST. AND I HAVE OTH... JOBS TO ATTEND TO.)

VON BRUCKEN TURNS AWAY FROM THE CABINE... SWISHING HIS CAPE AGAIN - HE LOVES TO DO T... UP ABOVE, LUNA USES A SMALL CAMERA TO PY... GRAPH THE TWO MEN AS THEY WALK OUT OF ... OFFICE.

VON BRUCKEN
(IF I INCREASE YOUR FEE WILL YOU PUT THIS OTHER WORK ASIDE?)

MYSTERY MAN
(PERHAPS)

THE END

YOU'RE READING THE WRONG WAY

This is the last page of *Amazing Agent Luna* Volume 1.

This book reads from right to left, Japanese style. To read from the beginning, flip the book over to the other side, start with the top right panel, and take it from there.

If this is your first time reading manga, just follow the diagram. It may seem backwards at first, but you'll get used to it! Have fun!